D0103882

TWO-PUTT GREENS IN 18 DAYS

A How-to Guide for the Weekend Golfer

WALTER OSTROSKE
PGA Teaching Pro

and JOHN DEVANEY

Photography by Aime La Montagne

A PERIGEE BOOK

Perigee Books
are published by
The Berkley Publishing Group
200 Madison Avenue
New York, NY 10016

Copyright © 1992 by Walter Ostroske and John Devaney
All rights reserved. This book, or parts thereof,
may not be reproduced in any form without permission.
Published simultaneously in Canada

Library of Congress Cataloging-in-Publication Data

Ostroske, Walter.
        Two-putt greens in 18 days: a how-to guide for
the weekend golfer / Walter Ostroske and John Devaney;
photography by Aime La Montagne.
                p.   cm.
        "A Perigee book."
        ISBN: 0-399-51747-2 (alk. paper)
        1. Putting (Golf) I. Devaney, John. II. Title.
III. Title: 2-putt greens in eighteen days.
    GV979.P8085   1992   91-30444 CIP
    796.352'35 — dc20
Cover design by Richard Rossiter
Cover photograph by Aime La Montagne

Printed in the United States of America
                7   8   9   10

This book is printed on acid-free paper.
                ∞

TWO-PUTT GREENS IN

18 DAYS

Also by the authors

Break 100 in 21 Days:
A How-to Guide for the Weekend Golfer
Correct the 10 Most Common Golf Problems in 10 Days

This book is dedicated to John Devaney. Without him this book and the others I have done could not have been written.

Walter Ostroske
Hempstead, New York

Contents

Contents

Two-Putt Greens: The Key to Golfing Happiness

You probably have heard dozens of reasons why putting is the most important part of golf. The two most obvious ones are:

1. *Putting is the Great Equalizer.*

   You are standing 20 feet away from the cup. Standing next to you is a low-handicap golfer, or even a pro. He or she is also 20 feet from the cup. You are as physically capable of stroking the ball into the cup as the low handicapper or the pro. He or she may knock the ball into or close to the hole more often than you, but on any one putt, you and the low handicapper or the pro are equals. This is not true from the tee, fairway or bunker, where physical skills such as hitting the ball longer and straighter do count. On the green the 250-yard hitter and the 150-yard hitter are equals.

2. *You must putt on every hole.*

   It's the rare hole where you don't putt. The one exception: if you hole out with a shot from a bunker or a fairway—and you know how often you do that. You may not use a driver or a long iron or even a short iron on some holes, but on 99 out of every 100 holes—at least—you must know how to use the putter. It is estimated, in fact, that at least 40 percent of all golf strokes are putts.

I am sure you have often reminded yourself about both of those truisms as you rued a three-putt green. But here's my number-one reason why putting is the most important part of your golf game:

Good putting can more than make up for a bad round while bad putting can ruin a good round.

Let's look at a good round. You drive the ball off the tee straight onto the fairway on every hole and at least half the time you land 10 to 15 yards longer than your usual distance with a driver. You hit the greens in regulation on at least half the holes, while on most rounds you are lucky when you make greenies once or twice a round. But you three-putted—or even four-putted—on each green that you landed on in regulation, greens where you had a good chance for birdie or par.

You go away mad—mad at yourself for blowing such golden opportunities. You came in with only your average score when you should have come in with a personal best at least five or six strokes below your average.

Now let's look at a bad round—at least it was bad from tee to green. You slam tee shots into woods,

Walter Ostroske and a
golfer's best friend.

and you scramble on almost every hole to get onto
the green with one stroke over regulation—that is,
three strokes on a par-four hole, four strokes on a
par-five hole. If you are a high handicapper, you
made it to the green two strokes over regulation.

But then—wonder of wonders!—your putter
turns into a magic wand. You waft in three or four
long ones from more than 20 feet, you sink a half-
dozen medium ones from 10 to 12 feet, and you

11

drop every short putt from five feet on in. You one-putt or two-putt each green. That takes anywhere from 8 to 12 strokes off your average number of putting strokes. You mark down one of your best scores—if not, indeed, your all-time best. At the 19th hole your partners are raving about your phenomenal putting, forgetting all about your wild drives into the woods.

And you go away gloriously happy.

You see what I mean. Good putting is the key that unlocks the door to golfing happiness.

I can give you that key. I have been teaching low-handicap and high-handicap golfers for more than 25 years as the head pro at the Hempstead Golf and Country Club on New York's Long Island. I've written two other books on golf, *Break 100 in 21 Days* and *Correct the 10 Most Common Golf Problems in 10 Days*. What I have found is that any reasonably coordinated man or woman, even those who play no more than a dozen times a year and mostly on weekends, can lower their scores by (1) listening to what I tell them and (2) practicing what I tell them.

For you, that means practicing your putting for about one hour a day for the next 18 days (and you can practice almost anywhere, including your living room or office). Do that and you are on the road to that golf heaven where there is never, never a three-putt green.

Choosing the Right Putter

You can buy an almost infinite variety of putters. Just like people, they come in all different sizes, shapes and weights. That makes sense, since putting is the most individualistic part of the game. There is no "right" way to putt any more than there is a "wrong" way to putt. But there are smart and dumb ways to putt. Choosing the putter that makes you feel most confident on a green could be the smartest move you'll ever make in golf.

Shown on the next page are the four most common kinds of putters as far as design is concerned. They are:

- The end-shafted putter, whose shaft is connected to the heel of the putterhead.
- The center-shafted putter, whose shaft is connected to the middle or sweet spot of the putterhead.
- The goosenecked or offset putter, whose putterhead is slightly behind the shaft.
- The mallet-head putter, which has a little bit more mass or weight in the head for added confidence.

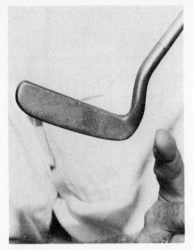

The end-shafted putter.

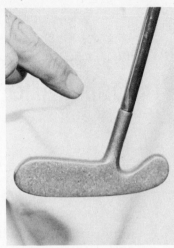

The center-shafted putter.

The goosenecked or
offset putter.

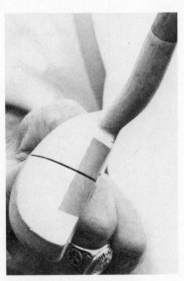

The mallet-head putter.

Looking at the shaft itself, there is the elongated shaft, which is so long that you don't have to bend over the ball. Elongated putters have become increasingly popular and might be right for you if you have back problems or if you see things better from a distance.

On the other hand, many golfers tell me that they feel more confident and in control of a putt when they hover close to the ball. Either they choke down on the shaft of a regular-length putter or they choose a shorter-shafted putter.

But keep this in mind: Putting is the most individualistic part of the game. So if you can roll the ball into the cup with a broomstick, show me where you buy those broomsticks.

But I do have three suggestions for you to consider when you are buying a new putter.

1. Putterheads come in varying weights. If you pick up a few in a pro shop, you will immediately feel the weight differences, even though one might be only a few ounces heavier or lighter than another. I personally feel that the heavier putterheads are preferable to the lighter ones. If you have more weight in the putterhead, you can take shorter strokes on long and medium putts; with less weight in the putterhead, you must take a longer stroke to cover the same distance. And the shorter the stroke, the fewer chances for error.

2. Buy a putter with a grip whose front side is

The elongated-shaft putter (left) and the standard-length putter (right).

flat. As you can see in the photo of my putter on this page, the flat side runs down the length of the grip. When you put your thumbs on the flat part, you know that the club has to be square to the target line. You don't have to look down the shaft to make sure that the putterhead is square; it has to be square if the thumbs can feel the flat part of the grip. When the grip is a round one, like the ones on all your other clubs, you must look down to see if the putterhead is square to the target line.

Walter's finger points to the flat front side of his putter shaft. His left hand grips a round-shafted putter.

The scored line on the putterhead indicates the sweet spot is directly behind the ball.

3. Buy a putter that has a line scored on the top of the putterhead to indicate the middle of the putterhead—that is, the sweet spot. As the photo shows, the line tells you that you have placed the putterhead's sweet spot exactly where it should be—directly behind the ball. Without that scored line, you can't be sure that the ball is in line with the sweet spot of the putterhead.

Now pick up your putter and let's talk about the grip and the stance.

Taking the Right Grip and Stance

THE GRIP

The putting grip is about as different from the grip for other clubs as the golf grip is from the grip for swinging a baseball bat.

First, grip the club with the left hand. As with the full-swinging clubs, the putter is held with the last three fingers of the left hand. It is very important that the left thumb is pointing straight down the shaft at the clubhead. As for the index finger, let's just leave it held away from the shaft for a moment.

Now for the right hand. We place the right hand on the putter a little differently than we would when gripping the other clubs. Put all the fingers on the grip, the pinkie finger included. Again, it is very important that the right thumb also be pointing straight down the shaft.

Now let's bring that left index finger into the

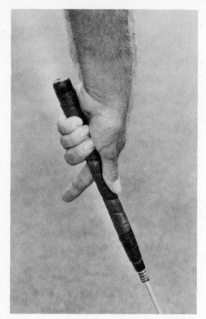

The left-hand grip.

putting grip. Bring that left index finger in to overlap the right hand so that the left index finger points straight down the shaft on a line that is parallel to the line formed by the two thumbs.

This is called the reverse overlapping grip. We use the overlapping grip for the full-swinging clubs, the right pinkie overlapping the first finger of the left hand. But when we putt, we do the reverse: The first finger of the left hand overlaps the pinkie and crosses the next three fingers of the right hand. That's because when we putt we want as much right-hand control as possible, the right hand being our dominant hand and thus the steadiest. (Left-handers, of course, should substitute left for right in all of the above.)

THE STANCE

There are some pros—Gary Player is the most notable—who like to putt with the ball lined up with the front foot. Others will line up the ball off the back foot.

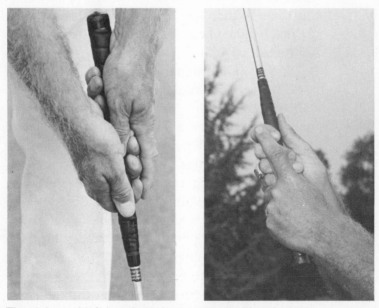

The right and left hands in the reverse overlapping grip.

But I tell both low and high handicappers that you are less likely to hit off-line if you center the ball between your feet. It is a familiar stance, hence a comfortable one; it's the stance we use for nearly all shots when the ball is on the ground (and not on a tee). Also, I believe that this stance gives us a better view of the ball during both the backswing and the through swing. And for a reason I will explain during Day Four, this stance gives you a gauge for determining the length of the backswing and the length of the through swing. Finally, this stance allows us to see that we are bringing the club back on a straight line and coming through to impact on that same straight line. In short, with this stance we are much more likely than with any other stance to hit the ball straight.

The feet should be parallel to the target line, not open-stanced (the front foot drawn back) or closed-stanced (the rear foot drawn back). I like to pretend that I'm standing on a floor carpeted with a large sheet of graph paper, or on a tiled floor where all the lines form squares. I want to feel that not only are my feet forming a parallel line with the target line, but my knees, hips and shoulders are also forming that same straight line that is parallel with the target line (see photo). If feet, knees, hips and shoulders form a line parallel with the line to your target, it is easier to keep the putterhead straight on that target line during the follow-through.

How close together should you keep your feet

The feet, knees and hips should be parallel to the target line.

when you putt? That depends on the distance you want the ball to travel. If it's a long putt (20 feet or longer), the feet should be about shoulder-width apart. If it's a medium-length putt (6 to 19 feet), the feet should be closer together, inside the shoulders. The gap between the feet becomes narrower as the putt's distance becomes shorter. If it's a short putt (within six feet), the feet are about a hand's width apart.

Golfers are always asking me, "Walter, how close should I stand to the ball when I putt?"

"We are all built differently," I answer, "but on a long or medium putt you should stand far enough away from the ball so that your arms and the clubhead can pass freely. Your body should not get in the way of the stroke."

More precisely, I stand about a foot away from the ball for a long putt, snuggling closer to maybe only four inches from the ball for a very short putt.

Of course, that doesn't answer the big question: Now that I have the putter I like and I am comfortable with the grip and the stance, how do I putt the ball?

My answer: Think of a grandfather clock. Let me explain that tomorrow.

Putting Like a Pendulum

Grip your putter at the top with the thumb and forefinger of your right hand. Now, with your left hand tap the middle of the shaft so that the club begins to swing back and forth. It will swing like the pendulum of a grandfather clock. It goes straight back and it comes straight through. What you are watching, as the clubhead swings in an arc—backward, downward, upward—is the pure pendulum motion, the motion you want to acquire for your pure putting stroke.

True, some pros will use a wristy kind of stroke. They use the wrists as the hinge for the swing. For the pendulum stroke the shoulders are the hinge. The trouble with the wristy swing is this: When the wrists are the hinge, you are much more likely to strike the ball on the upswing. That uppercut stroke will multiply anything that has gone wrong up to that point. For example, if you impact the ball with too much oomph, the uppercut motion will add more oomph. Similarly, if you impact the ball with the putterhead turned left or right on a

25

The putterhead swings like the pendulum in a grandfather clock.

It swings the same distance each way.

The wristy stroke.

straight putt, the uppercut motion will throw the ball even more left or right. And even when you have done everything right up to impact, the ball that is hit with an uppercut motion is more likely to come up short of the hole because it will not have good end-over-end roll. Finally, on a putt that must break left or right, the ball hit with an uppercut motion is more likely to veer even more sharply left or right, again because it lacks true end-over-end roll.

You get that end-over-end roll with a pendulum swing because the mass of the clubhead meets the ball squarely. Unlike the uppercut, which is a decelerating stroke, the pendulum stroke provides accelerating motion and, as a result, true end-over-end roll.

Good putting comes down to this: Take the putter away from the ball on a straight line. Bring the club forward on a straight line to impact the ball. Follow through on a straight line toward the target, as the photos below show. The ball will roll on a straight line to the target—whether the target is the cup or the point where you want the ball to slow down and break toward the cup.

As you hold your putter with your right thumb and index finger and allow it to swing like a pendulum on its own as you did at the beginning of this

Take the putterhead back on a straight line, bring the clubhead forward on a straight line before and after impact.

lesson, you will see that the clubhead will swing to the right side at just about the same speed as it does to the left. It doesn't swing slowly to the right, then hurry to the left. It is a leisurely and controlled swing from start to finish.

You want to feel that same leisurely and controlled motion when you putt—the motion of a pendulum inside a grandfather clock. Like that pendulum, you are in no hurry. You take the putterhead back slowly, you bring it to impact slowly, you follow through slowly. I see too many golfers bring the putter back slowly, true enough; but then

The pendulum swing: It's slow, controlled, and travels at the same pace going back as it does coming forward.

I see them start to think: "Hey, I am not going to hit this ball hard enough." So they hurry up the swing and jab at the ball, sending it off the target line.

Here are the key words to remember: A pendulum swing is *slow* and *controlled*, going *the same distance* backward that it comes forward, and it travels at the *same leisurely rhythm and pace* on the through swing as it traveled on the backswing. If the putterhead went 15 miles an hour toward your back foot, it must travel at 15 miles an hour toward the front foot.

DRILLS FOR THE PENDULUM STROKE

1. Hold the butt end of the putter with the thumb and first finger of your right hand so that the putterhead is about a foot off the ground. Start it swinging with your left hand and keep it swinging for about 15 minutes, impressing on your muscle memory that the clubhead goes straight back, moves straight ahead and sets its own pace. Like the pendulum of a grandfather clock, it never changes pace, and it is never in a hurry.

2. Place a ball equidistant between your feet. Stand over the ball with a putter. Take the putter straight back, then bring it forward. You will see that when the putter's shaft is exactly at a right angle to the ground, the clubhead makes contact

with the ball. This is the bottom of the pendulum's arc. Do this for about 15 minutes without aiming at a target or thinking about the speed or direction of the putt. Get the feeling of the pendulum motion you observed and felt when the club was swinging between your fingers.

3. Swing the club between your thumb and forefinger for a minute or two, then tap four or five balls with the putter. Go back to swinging the club between your fingers for another minute or two, then again tap four or five balls with the putter. Relate for your muscle memory the pendulum motion you observed when the club was swinging between your fingers with the pendulum motion you should feel when you go through your putting stroke. Alternate the two exercises for about 30 minutes.

Making the Ends Match Up

I see a lot of high handicappers—and even some low handicappers—make this mistake, especially on the shorter putts of two feet or less: They bring back the clubhead slowly, say to a line with their back toe. But just after they impact the ball, they stop the stroke. They jab or stab at the ball. They fear they are going to strike the ball so hard that it will run over the hole. They fail to make the distance of the back end of the stroke match the distance of the front end of the stroke. And that can be fatal for both speed and direction.

What makes this jabbing habit especially perilous to your putting health? Often when you jab or stab or quit on a short putt, the ball does pop into the hole. You may begin to jab at all of the short and medium putts. Almost inevitably, you will be committing the most common fault of high handicappers—leaving putts short of the hole, two-putting to cover a distance of perhaps no more than 24 inches.

To determine if you are a jabber, ask a friend to

The jabbing stroke: The clubhead passes the back foot on the backstroke but fails to clear the front foot on the follow-through.

stand behind you while you putt for 10 or 15 minutes. On all of your long or medium putts your friend should see the putterhead come past your back foot on the takeaway and past your front foot on the through swing.

Here is a tip I have found most effective in teaching golfers to make the two ends of the pendulum putting stroke match up:

During my pre-putt routine (which we will talk about at tomorrow's session), I decide that for a putt of a certain length, I need a force that will require my putterhead to come into line with the heel of my back foot. After impact I concentrate on bringing the putterhead to a point where it is exactly on line with the heel of my front foot.

Remember: You are copying the swinging motion of the pendulum in a grandfather clock. When did you ever see a clock's pendulum swing 18 inches to the right but only 12 inches to the left?

DRILLS TO MAKE THE ENDS MATCH UP

I believe that by showing your subconscious the right thing to do, you will impress on your muscle memory the proper golfing mechanics—in this case, how to make the ends match up.

1. As you did in yesterday's drill, take your putter and hold it like a pendulum, gripping it with the right thumb and forefinger. With your left hand start it swinging. Looking down at the swinging putter you will see the clubhead swing past your back foot or toe and then complete the arc of its swing by moving past your front foot or toe. Watch this pure pendulum swing for 15 minutes, relating it as we did yesterday to the pure putting stroke.

2. Take a putter, stand over an imaginary ball and duplicate that pendulum swing. Think only pendulum, not putting, as you bring the putterhead past the back foot on the takeaway, past the

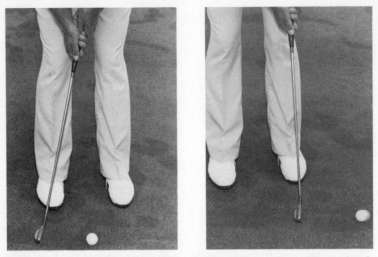

Making the ends match up: The clubhead is on line with the back toe on the takeaway; the clubhead is on line with the front toe on the follow-through.

front foot on the follow-through. Do that for 15 minutes.

3. Now place a golf ball betwen your feet and do the same thing, bringing back the putterhead to the right toe or the right heel, then coming forward with the putterhead to impact the ball, making sure the putterhead reaches the left toe or the left heel on the follow-through. Don't worry about direction or speed but just tap balls, keeping one thing in mind: Make the ends match up.

The Pre-Putt Routine: Keeping a Checklist for Accuracy

Before we ever swing a putterhead at a ball, we must first judge how hard we want to strike the ball—speed—and where we want to strike it to—direction.

Here is what I do as I walk onto the green, the putter in my hand. I begin to check off a list of things to do. The first is to walk to a point behind my ball. I look at the line from ball to target from my full height. I don't bend or crouch to look at the line; standing upright, I can tell much more easily whether this will be a straight putt or a putt that will break left or right to the hole. And from this vantage point, I can also determine much more easily than from a crouch how the green slopes. I now know whether this will be an uphill putt, a downhill putt or a sidehill putt.

As I stand behind the ball, I am also judging the

distance from my ball to the target. If I am not sure of the distance, I pace off the distance on a line parallel to my actual line. I know that one of my strides is equal to three feet. Find out the length of your stride and you will have your yardstick. When pacing off that distance to the left or right of my target line, I will also be taking another look at the slope of the green—this time from the side—to see whether I am putting uphill, downhill or sidehill, and whether or not the putt will break.

Next on my checklist is to remind myself what I learned on the practice green before I started the round. Before I tee off, I always take at least a dozen to two dozen strokes on the practice green. I recommend strongly that you practice on the putting green before a round; the practice green is like a barometer that will tell you what the greens are like on a given day—for example, if they are fast or slow. Greens are living, growing things; they change from day to day, even from hour to hour. If you are playing on a humid evening, the greens will be slower than three hours earlier, when the wind and sun were drying the greens, making them faster.

Remembering what I have "read" on the practice green as well as what I have read on this green, I get the answers to two questions: (1) How firmly should I hit the ball to roll the ball to the target? (2) Should I stroke the ball straight to the cup, or should I aim for a spot on the green where I expect the ball will break toward the cup? (On Day Six I will explain how to read greens for speed and direction.)

I now stand over the ball, placing my putterhead behind the ball to make sure that the ball is lined up with the sweet spot of the putterhead. My checklist continues as I make sure that the putterhead is neither open nor closed but square to the target line. (See photographs at the bottom of the page and at the top of page 40.) Next I make sure that my feet, knees and shoulders are on a line that is parallel with my line to the target.

Now, with nose and chin on a plumb line over the ball, I swivel my head between the ball and the cup,

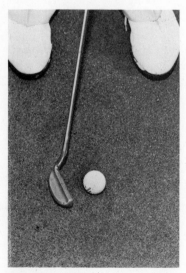

Closed clubface.

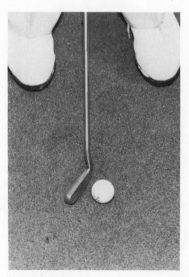

Open clubface.

Square clubface.

checking distance and line one last time. I am looking at where I want to roll the ball, either straight to
the cup or to a target point where I want the ball to
slow down and let gravity carry it down to the cup.
My eyes are backtracking along that line to the ball.
Then, when I feel comfortable that I have judged
how firmly I should hit the ball along that line, I
take the putterhead back slowly on a straight line to
begin the stroke.

Let's say I made my approach putt and I knocked
the ball two feet from the cup. I move toward the
ball from behind, and I go through exactly the
same checklist routine:

☐ 1. Standing upright, I check distance and
line.

Checking distance and line from a point behind the ball.

☐ 2. Line up the sweet spot on the putterhead with the ball.

☐ 3. Make sure my grip is right, my knees and shoulders are square to the intended line.

☐ 4. Swivel my head to backtrack along the target line from target to ball.

☐ 5. Make my final judgment on the firmness of the stroke and on the line to the target.

☐ 6. With nose and chin on a plumb line over the ball, I putt.

I will go through that same checklist routine on every putt—long, medium or short—and on every hole of every round.

Avoid second-guessing yourself and changing your mind during the pre-putt routine. First of all, you should not stand over a putt so long that you have the time to change your mind. In golf, as in so many other things, first impressions are usually the right impressions. Go through the routine in checklist fashion, consolidate everything into a decision on speed and line, then putt.

If I do have a second idea as I stand over the ball, swiveling my head between the ball and the target, I step back away from the ball and start my checklist all over again from the beginning. I am not

Swiveling the head to backtrack along the target line.

Nose and chin on a plumb line over the ball.

changing my mind in the middle of my routine. I am starting all over to get a fresh new look.

DRILLS FOR THE PRE-PUTT ROUTINE

1. Drop four balls at varying distances from the cup, whether on a practice green or in your living room. Place one ball so that it is a short putt of less than four feet, the second so that it is an intermediate putt between short and medium (4 to 10 feet). Place the third a medium distance from the cup (10 to 20 feet) and the fourth a distance that would be rated a long putt (25 feet or more).

Now stand behind the fourth ball and judge the distance. Pace off the distance to see how accurately you judged the distance. Do the same for the medium, the intermediate and the short putt. You will be sharpening your judgment for distance. Do this for about 15 minutes, changing the positions of the balls and their distances from the cup.

2. Holding your putter, bend over a ball that is about one foot from the cup. Try to pretend that you are not only sinking the ball, but that you want to "sink" the putterhead, too. Push the ball toward the hole with the putterhead, following the ball with the putterhead so that you drop the ball into the cup and cross the putterhead over the cup. By

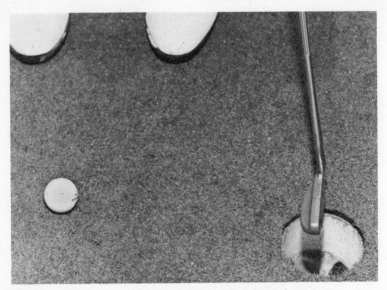

Imagine that you are sinking the putterhead on short putts.

imagining that you are sinking the putterhead with the ball, you will impress on your muscle memory the need to keep the putterhead square to the target line on those one-foot putts, the ones you should never, never miss. Do this for 15 minutes.

Reading the Greens

We read a green, as I said yesterday, for speed and direction. Now I already know something about the green's speed, even if this is hole number 1, because I have stroked putts on the practice green and that green has told me if the grass is damp (slow green) or dry (fast green). I look at the height of the grass on this green and if I see it has been mowed recently, I know that this green is going to be faster than others.

Now I also look at the grass between my ball and the cup. If I see that the grass looks shiny, it means the grain of the grass is going away from me—the blades are bending toward the cup. Since the blades are bending toward the cup, the ball will meet less resistance as it rolls—thus, shiny grass means a faster green. Conversely, if the grass has a darker shade, it means that the blades are bending toward my ball. If the blades are bending toward the ball, the ball will meet more resistance as it rolls. Hence, this green is going to be a slower green.

Finally, as far as speed is concerned, I judge—and this is the easiest part of reading a green—

whether the putt will have to roll uphill or downhill or whether it will be level. If this is an uphill putt, I will have to hit the ball with more firmness than I would hit a level putt. If this is a downhill putt, I will want to hit it with less force, since the downhill slope will add speed.

Now let's judge direction. If the path to the cup is level, then my target is the cup or a four-foot-wide circle around the cup. (I will explain why tomorrow.) I will aim for that circle or cup.

But if my ball sits on a slope so that the ball is above the cup or below the cup, I must judge how it will break so that it will curve into the cup from the high side. I must pick a spot where I want the ball to slow down so much that the slope will almost literally push the ball down to the cup. In short, I want gravity to take over and carry the ball downward to the cup.

What I do now is what the pros call "borrowing." I look at the slope on which my ball sits. How steep is the slope? If the slope is very steep, I am going to have to do a lot of borrowing. That means I must borrow, say, two feet of slope between the cup and an imaginary cup (or spot) above the cup. Defined another way, borrowing two feet means I figure the ball will begin to break at a spot two feet above the cup. I want the ball to slow down at that spot so gravity can carry it down to the cup.

On the other hand, if the slope is a slight one, I judge the slope will carry the ball downward only a

On steep slopes, aim for an imaginary cup or spot (the cluster of balls) well above the real cup.

On slight slopes, aim for the imaginary cup or spot (the cluster) close to the hole.

foot. So I borrow only a foot of grassy slope. Only practice is going to teach you how much or how little grass you need to borrow on breaking putts. As part of today's lesson, I am going to give you drills that will help you to read greens for speed and direction.

But you can "go to school," as we say, and learn how much or how little to borrow—how much or how little the ball will break—by watching how someone else's ball breaks as it rolls along the same side of the green where your ball sits. You can also "go to school" on the speed by watching how fast or how slow the ball rolls.

Let me note here that even when you are not on a green, you can "go to school" to learn about a particular green's speed and breaks. While you are waiting on a tee or fairway, observe what's happening on a nearby green; the pros do this all the time. You can see how balls roll to the cup from various sides of the green—sides from where you are likely to be putting later during your round.

Let's say I judge that I need to borrow 18 inches from the left side of the cup. That is, the ball will start to break downward at a spot 18 inches above the cup. I now aim at an imaginary cup that is 18 inches to the left of the real cup, that is, 18 inches above the cup. If I stroke the ball with the correct speed and on the correct straight line, the ball will "sink" into the imaginary cup, meaning that it will be traveling so slowly as it passes over that imaginary cup that gravity will carry it downward 18 inches into the real cup.

A cautionary word here: On shorter putts that break, we must be careful not to hit the ball so firmly that the ball "goes through the break," as the pros say. The ball travels so fast over the imaginary hole that gravity can't grab it or, put another way, the slope can't take charge and push the ball down into the real hole.

On very short breaking putts, say those within two or even three feet of the hole, it's often wise, especially on slightly slanted slopes where there is only a break of a few inches, to ignore the break. That is, aim for the real hole and putt straight, hitting the ball so firmly that the ball goes through the break and into the hole.

DRILLS FOR READING GREENS

1. Stand behind a ball that's about 25 feet from the cup on a practice green and judge the distance and direction you need for the putt. Then roll a ball as you would a bowling ball—don't pitch it—to the cup in the direction and with the firmness you would use if you were putting. See how far the ball goes and whether it rolls in the direction you judged it would roll. Did it go straight or did it

break? Was it short (bad!) or long (better!)? How close to the cup did it stop? Now, based on what you learned, putt the ball to the cup. Do this for about 30 minutes, alternating between rolling the ball to the cup and putting it. You will build confidence in your ability to read greens for speed and direction—and confidence is another name for accurate putting.

2. Stand about 20 feet from a cup that has a sidehill break. The ball must break downward right to left a certain distance above the cup. Judge how much distance you must borrow to make the ball break into the cup. Roll a ball so that it breaks downward right to left toward the cup. See how close you come to the cup. Then take a putter and, borrowing more or less depending on how the rolled ball broke, putt the ball so it breaks to the cup. Alternate rolling the ball and putting for five minutes.

Now pick up your putter and, standing about 20 feet away, putt 12 balls so that all 12 balls drop into the hole on either the first or second putt.

3. Go to the other side of the hole and roll the ball from about 20 feet away so that it breaks downward left to right to the cup. Repeat the rest of drill number two.

4. Find a hole with an uphill slope and judge how firmly you must roll the ball from about 20 feet

away so that it rolls uphill and into the cup. Then roll three or four balls toward the cup. Based on how close you came to the hole with those rolled balls, use the proper firmness to tap balls to the hole. Sink 12 straight putts from 20 feet away in either one or two strokes.

5. Go to the downhill side of the hole and repeat drill number four.

Think Four Feet,
Not Four Inches

You are standing anywhere from 20 feet to 40 or 50 feet from the cup. This is the long putt, a putt that even the pros sink fewer than once in 20, 30 or more tries. You are not aiming to sink this putt, although if you are skillful enough and lucky enough—luck being the more likely part—to drop the putt, that's a bonus. It will make up for the one you missed from two feet on the last hole. But while you can't expect to sink this long putt, neither should you even dream of taking three putts to cover this long distance. Three putts are not the reason why you bought this book nor the reason why I am writing it. Let's banish three putts from your life.

When I teach golfers how to roll an approach putt, such as anything more than 20 feet, I first take six or seven balls and place them in a semicircle around the cup, leaving open a pathway to the cup. The semicircle is about four feet in diameter. I tell the golfers: "That's your target, not a four-and-a-quarter-inch-wide hole but that 48-inch-wide circle." I have expanded their target 12 times.

I remind them that while they should aim for that wide circle, if they knock the ball into that four-inch hole, that's great, that's a grand-slam home run. But they have also hit a home run if they can hit the ball within the circle. Then they face a second putt of two feet or less, a putt they are much more likely to make than miss, for a two-putt green.

After I see that a golfer is hitting the ball within that four-foot circle at least three out of every four times, I add this refinement: I tell him or her: "You have hit a perfect approach putt if your ball stops anywhere within that circle, but some approach putts are more perfect than other approach putts. If your putt goes past the hole and then stops within the circle, that's a better putt than one that stops within the circle but comes up short of the hole."

The reason, of course, has been heard more than once by every golfer, but it is a truism that bears repeating: Never up, never in. That is, if your putt stops short of the hole, it has no chance of going in, but if it goes past the hole, it at least had a chance to drop.

Nearly all high handicappers commit the same fault: hitting their putts short of the hole. Almost always—when we get to uphill and downhill putts I'll give you some exceptions to this rule—it is better to aim your putts to go past the hole rather than to stop short of the hole.

When you go to a practice green or when you practice at home, get into the habit of aiming your long or medium putts at a circle that is four feet wide for the long putts, two feet wide for the medium putts.

On practice greens I see golfers trying to hole out their long putts. They sink one of maybe 20 or 30, and go away mad. There are few things in this game more disheartening and discouraging than a poor practice-putting session.

And that's bad for at least two reasons. First, you are so discouraged that you are less likely to practice putting as often as you should, which is every day if at all possible. And an unsuccessful practice-putting session will weaken confidence in your putting, and confidence is the name of the putting game.

But if you practice your putting by aiming for a wider (and thus easier to make) target, and you say to yourself, "If I sink half of these putts, I will have a terrific session," then you are going to go away eager to practice again and more confident about your putting.

DRILLS FOR "CIRCLE" PUTTING

Keeping in mind that you are always aiming at an expanded target, place six balls in a line 25 feet to

Practice putting balls to stop within a four-foot-wide semicircle around the cup.

35 feet from the cup on your carpet or on a practice green. Using a half-dozen or so balls, form a semi-circle around the cup with an opening for your putting path. The semicircle should be four feet wide. Tap the nearest ball toward the circle, then the next. If three balls miss the circle, restore the line of six balls and start over again. When you knock four of six balls into the circle three times in

a row, reduce the width of the circle to three feet and repeat the drill. Don't finish until you have placed four of six balls within the circle three times in a row.

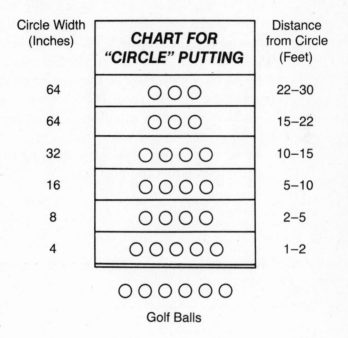

Circle Width (Inches)	CHART FOR "CIRCLE" PUTTING	Distance from Circle (Feet)
64	○ ○ ○	22–30
64	○ ○ ○	15–22
32	○ ○ ○ ○	10–15
16	○ ○ ○ ○	5–10
8	○ ○ ○ ○	2–5
4	○ ○ ○ ○ ○	1–2

○ ○ ○ ○ ○ ○

Golf Balls

For a second drill, see the chart above. Place the half-dozen or so balls in a semicircle that's four inches wide. Then, from one to two feet away, putt six balls at the four-inch-wide semicircle. You should roll five of the six balls inside that semicircle. Then form a semicircle that's eight inches wide and putt the six balls from two to five feet away. You should roll four of the six within the eight-inch-wide semicircle. Now form a semicircle that's 16 inches wide. From 5 to 10 feet away, you should roll four of the six balls within that 16-inch-wide circle. Next form a semicircle 32 inches wide and putt from 10 to 15 feet away. You should also roll four of the six within the semicircle. Now form a semicircle 64 inches wide. From 15 to 22 feet away, knock three of the six balls within that semicircle. Finally, keeping the semicircle at 64 inches, putt six balls from 22 to 30 feet away and again roll three of the six within the 64-inch semicircle.

Remember: Your ultimate goal is to turn the widest green into a two-putt zone.

DAY EIGHT

Aiming for a Target

Whether you are looking at a long putt that is 30 feet from the cup, or a medium putt that is 15 feet from the cup, you face a problem: As you bend over the ball, your peripheral vision is not wide enough for you to see the cup. You can't see your target.

Trying to hit a target you cannot see as you impact the ball creates obvious problems: How can you hit a bull's-eye you can't see?

Solution: spot or target putting. It's akin to what you do when you bowl. A bowler runs up to the line and aims at a spot marked on the lane a foot or so in front of the line. He tries to roll the ball over that spot, knowing that if the ball passes over the spot, the ball is rolling on the line to his target.

But bowling lanes are marked with spots or diamond-shaped marks to show where you should groove the ball. There are no spots or diamonds on putting greens. You must find a spot—a dark patch, a yellow straw, anything that stands out— that is on the line to your target and within two or three feet of your ball. It lies within range of your

Aim for spots along your target line that are close to you, such as the two coins placed here to demonstrate spot putting.

peripheral vision. When you roll the ball over that spot, you know you have started the ball on the correct line to your target.

If you're lucky, you may see two spots on the grass that sit on either side of your putting line. Now you can roll the ball between those two spots, as you would kick a ball between the uprights of a football goalpost. If the ball rolls through that "gateway"— which is on a line to your target—again you know you have started the ball on the correct line to your target.

When you are looking at a medium putt of 10 to 15 feet, picking one spot about two or three feet away may be the only spot you need. But for longer putts, I recommend that you pick two spots—and only two. One should be about two or three feet away, the other about 10 feet from you—and therefore inside your peripheral-vision range.

To sum up: For long putts, when you roll the ball across the first spot—or through the "goalposts" that straddle your line—you know that your putt has started on the correct line, since the spot or the "goalposts" are sitting on the target line. When the ball also crosses over the second spot, you know you have hit the ball firmly enough to keep it on that straight line to your target.

With spot or target putting, you are no longer aiming blind. That's one reason why spot putting is a must for accuracy on long and medium putts.

Roll the ball between two spots that straddle your target line.

And spot putting gives you the same advantage as putting to a four-foot circle: It expands the bull's-eye. You are not aiming at a target as far away as 30 feet. You are aiming at a target perhaps only two feet away, and at another target perhaps only 10 feet away. Obviously, it is a lot easier to hit a bull's-eye two feet away than a bull's-eye 30 feet away.

I recommend spot or target putting even for a putt as short as three to six feet. I recommend it for the same reason I recommend spot putting for medium and long putts: It's a lot easier to hit a target a foot away than a target six feet away.

DRILLS FOR TARGET OR SPOT PUTTING

1. Take three quarters and place the first about two feet from your ball, the second four feet, the third six feet away. Strike 10 balls so that all 10 balls cross the first quarter, more than half cross the second quarter and at least three cross the third quarter. If you don't equal those numbers with your first 10 balls, put down another 10 balls and keep trying until you do.

2. Go to the other side of the cup and repeat drill number one.

3. Stick two tees into the green about four inches apart. Place 10 balls in a row about six feet behind the tees. Putt each ball so that it runs through the "goalposts." Knock at least six of the 10 balls between the tees.

The Texas Wedge: Handle With Care!

The Texas wedge is not a wedge at all, of course, but your putter. The putter becomes the Texas wedge when it is used to putt the ball from the collar or the apron of the green. The term "Texas wedge" came to golf from Texas, where hot and dry summers scorch fairways, leaving bald spots or grass so thin you can putt the ball across these areas around the greens and it will roll as evenly as it would roll on a green.

But even when the grass on an apron or collar is thick many golfers like to use their putter to ram the ball onto the green, and then hope it will roll to the cup. Many of those golfers have no confidence in their chipping game. They feel much more confident when they are holding a putter, so they use the Texas wedge. And I tell them that they are right. When you are in the scoring zone, always choose the club you feel most comfortable using.

But you can risk your scoring health when using the Texas wedge, the most likely danger being that you will ram the ball so hard onto the green that the ball will overshoot the hole and you'll need two or even three more putts to hole out.

You can make that less likely to happen, however, by adopting this rule: Never use the Texas wedge when you are more than three feet off the green. Better still, never putt if you are more than one foot off the green.

Many golfers find the Texas wedge a handy tool when their ball sits on the collar on a steep slope that runs up or down to the green. They would prefer to roll the ball up or down the slope rather than trying to get the ball airborne with a chip, because chipping is difficult when you are standing on a slope with one foot above or below the ball. Both high handicappers and some low handicappers fear that a chip shot will land short of the green. But they are confident they can putt onto the green, even if they end up well past the pin, which is what usually happens, even on greens that slope uphill.

To use the Texas wedge with minimum risk, use the same putting stroke that you would use on the green except you must close the clubface slightly, hooding it; keep your hands slightly ahead of the ball. With your hands ahead of the ball and the putterface hooded, the ball will hop 6 to 12 inches after impact. It will fly over all or much of the thick grass that can slow it down or deflect it. On landing, it will roll as it should—end over end—toward your

Using the Texas wedge:
Clubface is closed slightly
and the hands are slightly
ahead of the ball. The ball
will hop when struck.

target. In short, you are using the putter to get the effect of a chip shot; the ball will be airborne a short distance, then roll a longer distance to the target.

To get as close to the cup as possible, aim for that four-foot circle that you aim for on all medium and long putts. And don't jab—that is, fail to follow through. A jab will almost always knock the ball off the target line. Just as for any other long putt, take a long backswing while keeping the putterhead straight on the line to the target, then match the length of the backswing with the length of the follow-through.

DRILLS FOR THE TEXAS WEDGE

1. Form a four-foot-wide circle of golf balls around the cup on a practice green. Crouch or kneel about a foot off the green, then roll a ball through the grass, just as you would roll a bowling ball. See how close the ball comes to the circle. Now, depending on whether you rolled the ball short or long, putt a ball with what you now think is the needed force to reach the circle.

Alternate between rolling a ball to the cup and putting a ball to the cup. Then putt 20 balls and try to get at least 15 of them into the circle. You will be

Use two clubs to make a backstop behind the cup. Putt from the fringe so the balls go past the hole but don't hit the backstop. Develop a touch so the balls stop short of the clubs.

getting the proper feel and touch for ramming a ball through thick grass onto a green.

2. Do the same drill from three feet off the green, again trying to putt 15 of 20 balls inside the circle.

3. Using two clubs, make a backstop about three feet behind the cup. Then, from about two feet off

the green, alternate between rolling a ball toward the cup and putting a ball toward the cup, hitting or rolling each ball so that the ball goes past the cup but does not strike the clubs, which would mean you overshot the hole. Then, after you have gotten the feel for getting the ball through the grass and just short of the clubs, try putting 10 balls so that at least seven roll past the hole but don't touch the clubs.

Thinking Direction, Thinking Speed

When you stand over a putt, as with any golf swing, it is not very helpful if you are thinking about all the things you must do. With the golf swing, I tell golfers to think of only three things: Bring the club up, bring the club down, bring the club through.

In the delicate art of putting, of course, thinking about doing too many things can cause the dreaded "yips," a twitching of the arms or hands that will knock your ball to hell and gone.

When you putt, you face two basic questions: What is my direction? What is my speed? You must decide on the line of the putt from your ball to the target, and you must decide how firmly or how softly you need to strike the putt.

Direction and speed.

Those are the two things you must think about. But on most medium or long putts, one must have priority over the other. If you give 50 percent of your concentration to one and 50 percent to the other, one or the other will not get the concentration it deserves for a particular putt.

Let me explain by showing you two different putts. Putt A is 20 feet long and you must roll the ball into a cup that is cut into the side of a slope. The ball must break downward to get into the cup.

I decide to pick a target area a foot above the cup where I want the ball to slow down to the speed I estimate will allow the slope to drag the ball toward the cup. If I hit the ball too firmly, the ball is going to speed over that target area; it will go through the break—and stop a long distance from the hole.

Obviously, then, both speed and direction are important: Roll the ball at a speed so it will break; direct the ball to the target area.

But seldom are they equal, especially with putts longer than 10 feet. If the putt is going to break, I must first make sure I am directing the ball into the target area; if it never reaches that target area, it can't break—and I have no chance of sinking the putt. If I get the ball into that target area, even if the ball is going a little too fast or a little too slow and the ball breaks to a greater or lesser degree than I had planned, the ball will stop close to the hole.

Conclusion: With breaking putts, direction takes precedence over speed. That is, I give maybe 60 percent of my concentration to direction, such as making sure I reach that spot a foot above the cup. I give 40 percent of my concentration to speed, reminding myself I want to cozy the ball into that area rather than ramming it into—and through—that area.

Now let's look at the second putt—putt B. This putt is a straight one of about 15 feet. I want to make sure I get the ball at least to the hole (never up, never in). Since the putt is straight, I know the line the ball will travel if my putterhead impacts the ball square to that target line. I can give 40 percent of my concentration to making sure I hit that ball square to the target line while giving 60 percent of my concentration to hitting the ball with enough speed so that it reaches the cup.

On most putts, the ratio is 60–40, 70–30 at the most. And on short putts of under 10 feet, the ratio should be 50–50. That's because I am aiming for a four-inch target. Direction is very important and so is speed since I want the ball to stop at that four-inch hole.

Suppose I face a long putt of 30 feet that I know will break about five feet above the hole. Now I am thinking 60 to 70 percent direction and only 30 to 40 percent speed. Why? Because I must direct the ball from a long way off to a narrow target area— that area five feet above the hole. Speed is important only in that I want the ball to enter that target area at a reasonably slow speed. But the ball must enter that target area if I am to have any chance of sinking my second putt. As far as speed is concerned, I am trying to coax the ball into the target area. But as far as direction is concerned, I must hit that target area five feet above the hole so the ball will break properly.

Now, remember, I am also thinking speed. If I hit the ball too fast, the ball will go through the break. If I hit it too slowly, the ball will never reach the break. But direction—getting the ball into the area where it will break—now takes at least a 60 to 40 percent priority over speed.

One last point: On straight putts I want to putt long rather than short, which is the big reason why I give speed priority over direction. I know the direction the ball will roll if it is struck correctly. But on curving putts we are really only guessing where the ball will begin to break. If the ball stops short of the hole because it lacked enough speed, that speed may have been slowed by the slope of the hill and not because of any fault of your own. In short, if you don't give enough speed to a breaking putt and it ends up short of the hole, you can't blame yourself completely, especially if your direction was good and you hit your target area. But if you don't give enough speed to a straight putt and your ball rolls straight for 15 feet and then stops inches short of the cup, you blew a chance to make a putt you normally don't make. You didn't concentrate hard enough on speed. But on a curving putt of 15 or more feet, which you can't expect to make, you have not hurt yourself nearly as much if you come up inches short of the hole.

To sum up: On long to medium straight putts, think mostly of speed to get to or past the hole. On breaking putts, think mostly of direction to get the ball *to an area close enough to hole out on your next putt.*

When you have a straight putt, be bolder with the speed factor. Charge on straight putts. When you stroke a curving putt, be more conservative with your speed. Use more of a coaxing stroke rather than a solid one. Think mostly of getting the ball to your target area, where it will break.

There are times to charge and times not to charge for the cup, but if you're wise, charge on straight putts, coax on breaking putts.

DRILLS FOR SPEED AND DISTANCE

Place six balls in a cluster on the uphill side of a green about where you think the ball will break down toward the cup. Place your ball about 10 feet from the cup. Roll the ball toward the cluster of balls. If your ball hits the cluster and scatters them, you rolled the ball with too much speed and the ball would have gone through the break.

Keep rolling balls until you can cozy five balls in a row to stop just short of the cluster. Now alternate

Alternately roll and putt balls at a cluster of balls. If your ball scatters the cluster, you rolled the ball too fast and the ball would have gone through the break.

between rolling and putting balls from six feet away. Roll balls so that at least four of every six come within an inch or two of the cluster. Then putt balls so that at least four of six stop within an inch or two of the cluster. Do the same drill from 12 feet away and from 18 feet away.

Place two balls two feet from each side of the cup. Putt balls from varying distances so they stop within the four-foot-wide circle.

What you are teaching your muscle memory is that on breaking putts, direction takes precedence over speed. But while direction is the more important factor—you want to reach the target area—speed is also important in that you don't want the ball traveling too fast as it enters that area.

For concentrating on speed in putting: Place two balls about two feet on either side of a hole. Then place four balls in a straight line to the cup 6, 12, 18 and 24 feet away (see photo). Putt each ball until you can stop three of four within that 48-inch circle. Bring the two balls in closer together by three to six inches, then knock three out of every four into that 36-to-42-inch circle.

Going Uphill, Going Downhill

We have already talked about sidehill putts, the ones where you use the slope of the hill to drag the ball downward to the hole. Today, let's talk about uphill putts and downhill putts.

If I had to make a guess, I would say that the places where weekenders are most likely to three-putt are on greens that require you to putt uphill or downhill. One reason for these three-putt greens on uphill and downhill lies is this: The weekender doesn't take enough time to study the severity of the slope of the green. If the slope is very slight going either uphill or downhill, the uphill or downhill putt is obviously not as difficult. The more severe the slope, the more difficult the putt as you try to decide how firmly you need to contact the ball. By not taking the time to study the slope, many golfers underestimate or overestimate the severity of the slope. Result: three putts. So I can't emphasize this too much: Take the time to study the slope when you face a downhiller or an uphiller.

Up to now, you may remember, I have been saying that it is nearly always wiser to be long instead of short on your putts. You probably remember the rationale for that rule: If you don't get to the cup, there is no way that you can drop the putt—never up, never in. The exception comes when you are putting uphill or downhill. Then you will often be wiser to putt short rather than long. You will understand why as I give you the four things to remember about uphill and downhill putts.

1. Uphill putts are easier to sink than downhillers. One reason: Because the putt has to go up the hill, we hit the ball firmly and thus it is more likely to stay on line from start to finish. By contrast, we are likely to stroke a downhiller a little easier and there is more of a chance it will roll off line. So, when you face a downhill putt, remember that while you don't want too much speed, you should tap the ball firmly, not in a wishy-washy way.

2. A downhiller is more likely than an uphiller to roll so far past the hole that you need at least two more putts to hole out. Therefore, you are better off being a little long rather than a little short on a downhill putt.

I give this as a rule: On medium or long downhill putts of 10 feet or more, the kind you are not supposed to sink but only get close enough to sink with the next putt, you are better off being long by a foot than short by six to eight inches. I would rather putt uphill from a foot away than putt downhill from half that distance.

3. On an uphill putt from 10 or more feet away, I want to place the ball in the bottom half of that 48-inch circle that I am aiming for—not in the top half. If the ball stops in the bottom half, leaving me short, I am putting uphill for my must-make second putt. If I am long, I face a much tougher downhill second putt.

4. On both downhill putts and uphill putts, it is very important that you hit the ball straight to the hole rather than to the left or right of the hole. Let's say you hit the ball straight on an uphill putt—but short. That's good. Let's say you hit the ball long on a downhill putt. That's also good. But the worst thing that can happen on an uphiller or a downhiller is this: You hit the ball to the left or right of the hole. Then you face a sidehill putt from a short distance away, and you have no idea how much the ball must break on a putt that you must sink.

I'll sum up by saying that on all first putts—uphill, downhill, sideways or straight—you should aim to stop the ball at the best position for your second putt. Think ahead. You want your second, must-make putt to be a comfortable one—as short and as straight as possible.

Place four balls so they form a box around the hole, each ball about a foot from the hole. For practicing uphill putts, try to tap each ball within the triangle formed by the cup and the balls marked A. For practicing downhill putts, try to tap each ball within the triangle formed by the balls marked B.

Thinking ahead is especially important when your first putt must travel uphill or downhill. You want your second putt to be not only short, but uphill, not downhill or sideways.

This tip, then, follows from what I have just told you: I will be a little bolder in going for the cup on my first putt downhill, because I know that if I roll the ball past the hole a little way, my second, must-make putt will be uphill. But I will be a little more cautious when my first putt is uphill. If I am short, I will have a relatively easy uphiller for my second putt; but if I am long, I face a tougher downhiller for my must-make putt.

DRILLS FOR UPHILLERS AND DOWNHILLERS

Form a box with four balls, each ball about a foot from the hole. Place 10 balls about 12 feet from the cup so that you are giving yourself a downhill putt. Now, putting downhill, putt at least eight of the 10 balls within the triangle formed by the cup and the balls farthest from you. In other words, roll the ball past the cup. Then place 10 balls about 12 feet from the cup on a slope so that you are now trying to make an uphill putt. Putting uphill, putt 10 balls so that at least eight of the 10 stop within the triangle formed by the cup and the two balls nearest you. In other words, stop the ball short of the hole so that your second putt is also an uphill putt.

Now move the four balls so they are about 18 inches from the cup and repeat this drill both uphill and downhill from 20 feet away. Then move four balls so they are about two feet from the cup and repeat the drill from 30 feet away.

Thinking Backboard
for Two-Footers

On most short putts, especially those within two feet of the cup, you want to putt straight, ignoring any break. From this distance, you don't need gravity to carry the ball to the cup. All short putts should be straight putts.

That means you must putt the ball firmly. If the ball is tapped too weakly toward the cup, it may roll the needed distance, but because it is rolling slowly, a blade of grass can turn it left or right, steering it away from the cup.

You want to tap the ball so firmly that it will roll fast enough to hit the back edge of the cup. To make sure I get the ball to the back edge of the cup, I aim for an invisible basketball-type backboard (see photo) set about an inch or two behind the cup. I want my ball to reach that backboard—and that insures I will hit the ball firmly enough for it to reach the back of the cup. And when the ball is hit firmly, it will roll fast enough to stay straight.

Aim for an imaginary backboard an inch or two behind the cup to get the proper speed for short putts.

To practice how to putt with firmness, knock over cups set to the left and right of the hole.

DRILL FOR BACKBOARD PUTTING

You can do this anytime and almost anywhere using practice-putting equipment, or you can do this on a practice green. Place two paper cups an inch or two behind the hole, one on the left and one on the right. Place 12 balls two feet away from the paper cup on the left. Tap all 12 balls so that they knock over the cup. If you miss on any putt, set up the 12 balls and start over again. Now place 12 balls two feet away from the paper cup on the right. Putt all 12 balls so they knock over the cup each time— again, start over if you miss any one of them.
h   Now place 12 balls two feet away from the hole. Swing with the same firm stroke you used to knock over the paper cups and drop 12 balls straight into the hole.

A Time Out

○ I want to take a breather here before we start on the lessons for Days 13, 14 and 15. So far I have been telling you how to putt like a mechanical man or woman. And I want to stress this point right here: The more robot-like and mechanical a putter you are—putting the same way each time with only the arms and hands moving—the more times you are going to score one-putt and two-putt greens.

○ But, happily, we are not robots. We are thinking people. Which means, of course, that our minds affect our putting. I have already mentioned how we use the thinking process to read greens. But the mind plays another role in putting.

○ Here's an example: Golfer A walks to a green and looks at a putt that must roll uphill about 20 feet and then roll sideways another five feet. "There is no way I can make this in less than three putts," he tells himself.

○ Golfer B has the same putt. He tells himself: "I'm going to sink this in maybe one, but certainly in no more than two putts." Golfer B almost always two-putts and sometimes he one-putts.

○ What's the difference between Golfer A and Golfer B? The difference is all in their minds— and in how they prepared for that tough putt. During the next three days I'll explain what I mean.

Getting That "Bet the Ranch" Confidence

In what situations are you most likely to three-putt a green? If you are like most low handicappers and high handicappers whom I see, you are most likely to three-putt when your approach shot lands anywhere from 25 to 40 or more feet from the pin, or when your first putt stops even as close as four feet from the cup. (If your first putt misses by 10 or more feet, you are almost certain to three-putt, and deservedly so: You have missed that four-foot-wide circle and must pay the penalty.)

Why are you most likely to three-putt when you face a very long putt or a relatively short putt? With the long putt, of course, you are confronted with another golf truism: The longer the distance, the less skill is involved and the more luck plays a role. My skill allows me to control a ball's speed and direction for the first three feet; after that I must cross my fingers or look up to the sky for help. Any hidden tuft of grass or slight slope or spike mark can alter the ball's speed and direction and that, as they say, is the luck of the green. So even though I strike a ball with a square blade and with the firmness or softness I think is needed, a ball that has to roll 10 or more feet may stop short of my target or roll past my target for reasons I can't control.

But having said that, I want to stress this: Skill can save you from most of the three-putt greens that are now inflating your score. Most of the time you should two-putt when you are 30 feet away and one-putt when you have hit your approach putt within 36 inches of the cup.

You should hole out at least 99 percent of the time when you are within 12 inches of the cup. Missing a 12-incher is shameful and nearly always a result of carelessness, slapping at the ball as though it were a gimmee (which it shouldn't be) or putting so quickly on this sure thing that speed or direction or both are wrong.

Now let's see how we can one-putt or two-putt in the three most common three-putt situations:

On those short 12-to-24-inch gimmees, tell yourself: "I am going to take my time. I am going to give this putt as much tender loving coaxing as I would give a 10-footer." Remember: A swing counts as one stroke whether you move the ball 250 yards or one inch.

On those long putts of 12 or more feet and on those short ones of 4 to 12 feet, adopt what I call the "I'll bet the ranch" attitude. Here's how to adopt that attitude:

Place a ball 12 inches from a cup. Bend over the ball with the correct stance and grip. Now take the proper pendulum putting stroke, making a full follow-through so that the putterhead crosses the cup as square as it was when it struck the ball, as though you were trying to drop the putterhead into the hole after the ball. The ball plunks into the cup. You will get the feeling that you can do this all day, knocking ball after ball into that cup, never missing. If someone asked you to knock a ball into the cup from this distance, you would "bet the ranch," if you owned one, that you would drop the ball into the cup.

Now stand 12 to 15 feet away from the cup. Your target is no longer that four-inch hole that you aimed at from 12 inches. Now your target is a much bigger bull's-eye—that four-foot-wide circle. And you are only a dozen or so feet farther away from where you stood when you had to aim at that four-inch hole.

Again stand over a ball. Taking the proper pendulum stroke with the front end matching the back end, tap the ball into that four-foot circle. As one ball after another rolls into that circle, you will get the feeling that you would bet that mythical ranch on your ability to tap at least eight of every ten balls into that big circle.

Now let me make my point here, a point I learned from a book on golf by the legendary Bobby Jones. It was Jones who pointed out that when we stand a medium distance from a cup—12 to 20 feet—we are very relaxed as we putt. This is our "comfort zone." We know we are not expected to knock the ball into the hole. We are expected only to tap the ball close enough so that we will be inches away for our second, sure-thing putt. There is no pressure. And being relaxed, we will usually not only get the ball close, we may even drop the ball into the cup.

Jones said, in effect, Why can't we have that same relaxed attitude when we putt from outside the comfort zone—that is, a long putt of 25 feet or a short putt of six feet? In both cases, we should tell ourselves that the target is as wide—four feet wide from 25 feet away, four inches wide from 36 to 72 inches away—as that four-inch target looked from 12 inches away. Phrased another way, the longer the putt, the bigger the target.

And now, having minimized the pressure by magnifying the target and having maximized your confidence with the feeling that you would "bet the ranch" on rolling this ball to your target, you will be walking away from two-putt greens instead of three-putting anywhere from three feet away to 30 feet away.

DRILLS FOR THAT "BET THE RANCH" CONFIDENCE

Place six balls around a hole so that each is six to eight inches from the cup. With the proper grip, stance and pendulum stroke, tap all six balls into the cup. If one misses, start over again and keep putting until you sink six in a row. As you putt these gimmees, you are instilling the belief that you could sink every six-incher you face.

Now place six balls about 12 feet from the cup. Tell yourself that you will putt six balls into a circle about 12 inches wide—a target three times bigger than the four-inch hole you were aiming to hit from six to eight inches away. And have the same confidence that you had when you were knocking in those six-inchers: While you are not going to sink these, there is no pressure on you because you are not expected to sink them. You only have to cozy the ball into a circle three times wider than the target you hit every time from six inches away. Knock six straight balls into that foot-wide circle.

Now stand 20 to 25 feet away. Aim for a circle around the cup that is about 48 inches wide. Remind yourself that you have magnified by four times the bull's-eye that you aimed at from half this distance. Putt six straight balls into that four-foot-wide circle. You will be instilling into your mind that every putt, no matter how long, is a gimmee just like those 12-inchers.

Repeat this to yourself: From six inches away, a target of four inches is a wide target. From 12 feet away, a target of 12 inches is a very wide target. And from 20 feet away, a target of 48 inches is a gigantic target.

You are eliminating most of the pressure. You are relating the confidence you felt when you were six inches from the hole to the confidence you now will feel as you think of every target as a huge bull's-eye. No longer will you try to squeeze the putt into a teeny-weeny target. Instead, remind yourself: The longer the putt, the wider the target. And if you would be willing to bet the ranch that you would sink 100 percent of those short six-inchers, you will soon be willing to bet the ranch that you will knock at least 80 percent of your medium-to-long putts into that widening circle. You are now on your way to erasing from your game the most common ways that golfers three-putt.

Games That Build Putting Confidence

Confidence is maybe the most important key to two-putting. If you believe you can sink that snaking 20-footer, you are perhaps half the way toward sinking it. Here are two putting games that I have devised to add confidence to your putting stroke.

You can play both games on a nine-hole putting green or on the carpet in your living room using paper cups or any of the many practice-putting devices that are available in pro shops.

GAME NO. 1

You are going to play nine holes. Par is two strokes for each hole, 18 strokes for the round. The rules for this game are: You can putt one, two, three or four balls at each cup, but you must putt the same number of balls on each hole. Let's assume that you decide to putt three balls on each hole. Since you have three chances to sink each of the putts, you win this game if you finish three strokes under par (15 strokes) for the round. If you had decided to putt four balls, you would win with 14 strokes or four under par. If you had used only two balls, the goal would be 16, or two under par.

You will understand how that scoring works in a minute. Place the three balls on the living-room rug or on the green about 20 to 25 feet from the cup (or at the starting point for the first hole if this is a practice-putting green at a golf course). Putt the first ball. Watch how it rolls to the cup—whether it rolls straight or whether it breaks and how it breaks and whether it ran long or short.

Using that knowledge, putt the second ball, aiming now to sink it. If you do, then you win. You one-putted the green and you are one under. If you fail to sink the second ball, try to sink the third. If the third one goes in, you have also won and your score is one under. If you miss all three balls, try to sink all three with your second putts. If you make one of the three, you have two-putted; you are even with par. If you miss all three of the second putts, then you are one over par; you've lost this hole, the course has won and you are four strokes away from your goal of finishing three strokes under par.

That second, short putt is as important in building confidence as the first long one. You are build-

Game No. 1: Having putted the first ball and seen it stop short of the hole, I putt a second ball, trying to sink it. If I sink the second, third or fourth ball, I have one-putted and I am one under.

ing confidence that you can sink those short second putts, the ones you must make to avoid the dreaded three-putt green.

There will come a day when you will have to sink one of those short ones while your knees are knocking. Winning or losing an important match—and maybe a lot of money—will hinge on that putt going in. Games like this will give you the confidence that you can make it.

Play each hole the same way, stroking three balls at each hole. Whenever you fail to sink a ball, knock the ball into the hole on the second putt. You are not only building confidence in your short-putting, you are making a habit of sinking the second putt. You are getting out of the habit of three-putting. And, of course, when you sink the first, second or third long putt, you are building confidence that you can sink the medium or long putts—the ones you are not expected to make.

GAME NO. 2

Place two balls on the ground. Putt the first ball, hoping to get it close to the hole but not so close that the ball drops. Then putt the second ball, aiming to get it into the cup (that's perfect). You are one under par. But you also win if the second ball stops

Game No. 2: Having putted the first ball, which stopped to the right of the cup, I tap a second, aiming to get it either into the cup or closer to the hole than the first putt.

closer to the hole than the first putt. Again you are one under. Play nine holes (or as many as time allows), trying to finish under par by fewer strokes than your personal best.

If your first putt rolls into the cup, you must then try to sink your second putt. But if you fail to sink the second, the penalty is only a par for the hole, meaning you are even, going neither under par nor over par for the hole.

Again, walk away from each hole only after sinking both balls, even if one is only an inch away. Never be casual on even the shortest putt of an inch or two. Never wave the club with one hand to swat at a short putt. Use the same pendulum motion to stroke the ball one foot that you would use for a 20-footer. You will keep that motion in the groove you want for all putts. And every time you hear that satisfying rattle of ball in cup, you are going to feel much more confidence in your stroke when you are looking at a 25-footer.

When the Confidence Comes Naturally

This will happen maybe once, at the most twice, during at least one of every two or three rounds you play. You land on a green, often after one of your best approach shots of the day, and you stand 20 to 30 feet from the cup. You see flashing neon lights that blink on a blade of grass: "Putt the ball to here and it will roll the rest of the way into the cup." Or a voice may whisper in your ear: "This is as sure a putt as that last one you sank from one foot away." I mean, I'm talking right now about the "Twilight Zone."

Listen to that voice, putt toward those lights. Go for it. Forget the circle of 48 inches and aim to hit that four-inch cup. If you've had a three-putt green earlier, this is your chance to make up for it with a one-putt green.

This intuitive feeling may be a matter of growing confidence. It usually happens in the middle of a round or during the back nine. Our confidence builds as putts roll into the cup.

Another explanation may be as simple as this: When you feel so confident that you are going to drop this son of a gun, you stroke the ball firmly, and firmly hit balls stay on line all the way to the cup.

Look, there are going to be plenty of greens where you won't feel at all confident. Let's say you must tap the ball uphill about ten feet so that it will then roll about ten feet downhill to the cup. That's tough—and no time to be bold. You must cozy that ball up the hill with just enough speed so gravity will pull it downhill—you hope. If you walk away with two putts on a slope like that, look up to the sky and say thanks.

But, conversely, just as there are times to be cautious, there are times to be bold. Sometimes you'll see this happen when you watch the pros on TV. They'll stand over a long putt, look one last time at the line, and you can sense that they are going to make it—and that they know they are going to make it. The ball will run to the cup as though it were drawn by a magnet.

There are no practice drills when you get into twilight zones. But I will conclude with this reminder: In putting, as in life, it's nearly always better to be safe rather than sorry, to be conservative rather than bold. But also as in life, there are times in golf to take chances and charge for it. And when blades of grass start talking to you, listen! Go for it!

Saving Strokes by Knowing the Rules of the Green

Not understanding the rules of the green can cost you more than your share of three-putt greens. Let's look at what the rules can do to save you strokes—or, if you don't know them, cost you strokes.

ATTENDING THE FLAGSTICK

When you are on the fringe off the green, where the grass is short or the ground bare, you may decide to use the putter as a Texas wedge and putt rather than chip. In that situation, you may leave the flagstick in the cup, using it as a target. If the ball hits the pin and the pin stops the ball from running past the hole, that's okay, even if the ball drops into the cup. There is no penalty for using

the pin as a backstop *as long as you are putting from off the green.*

But that's a no-no when you putt on the green. Then you must lift the pin out of the hole before you putt. Or you must ask a friend or a caddy to hold the flagstick and lift it out of the hole if the ball seems likely to strike it. If the ball does strike the pin, that's a two-stroke penalty in stroke or medal play, the loss of the hole in match play.

I recommend that you take out the pin for short putts, but ask a friend or a caddy to hold the pin for longer putts, when you need a target.

MOVING THE BALL

You may pick up the ball off the green to clean it. You may also pick up the ball when your ball sits on the putting line of another golfer who is away. He must putt before you. Take a coin or some other marker and place it directly *behind* your ball and then remove your ball. If the other golfer fears that the coin will knock his ball off line, you may then move the coin a clubhead or a clubshaft (or

You may leave the pin in the hole when putting from the apron or fringe with your Texas wedge.

You must take out the pin or have it attended by a friend when putting from on the green.

whatever distance you choose) to the left or right of the line. After the other golfer has putted, you then move the ball back to its original position, using the clubhead or the clubshaft to make sure you place the ball in its exact original position. Placing the ball closer to the hole than where it was is a violation of the rules that could cost you penalty strokes.

IMPROVING THE PUTTING LINE

You are allowed to repair the small craters punched into the green by crash-landing approach shots. You may take a tee or some other tool, such as a key, and jab under the crater with the tool's pointy end to lift up those craters or other kinds of ball marks to make them level. But the rule book doesn't allow us to repair spike marks. To my mind spike marks should be in the same category as ball marks— they're just as likely to throw a putt off line or slow it down—but up to now the rules people have said yes to ball marks, no to spike marks.

You may pick up loose objects such as broken blades of grass, straw or other wind-blown debris. But you may not remove anything that is connected to something else, such as a blade of grass that is connected to its roots.

You may move your ball when there is a visible

With a pointy instrument such as a tee, you are allowed to flatten out craters caused by the impact of approach shots.

puddle of water ("casual water" in the rule book) between you and the target. The ball may be moved to where there is a dry line to your target. But, again, you may not move the ball closer to the target or the pin.

WAITING ON "HANGERS"

When a ball hangs on the edge of the cup, seeming ready to drop at any moment, you may wait for the ball to drop—but you may not wait all day. In fact, you may not wait even a minute; the rule states you may wait only "a few seconds" and then you must putt out.

Finally, here are some rules of etiquette to keep in mind on the putting green. Don't walk around or make any other motion when someone else is putting, even though you may not be in his or her direct line of sight. Don't stand directly behind or directly in front of the person putting because your presence or your shadow may be disturbing. Always step over someone else's line from ball to cup so you leave no foot marks. If another player putts to a spot very close to the hole, within two feet, and then says, "I'll putt out," both etiquette and the rules allow him or her to do so, even though you are away and technically should putt first. But if the other golfer's approach shot lands closer to the hole than yours, you're away and the rules say you should putt first. But you can permit the other golfer to hole out if he or she asks.

I'll finish with this tip on etiquette that can make the difference between a one-putt green and a three-putt green for you or your fellow players. Take your time putting—but don't take too much time. The longer you take—lining up a putt, getting set, then hovering over the putt—the more tension you create in your hands and arms. Hovering too long over a putt almost always leads to doubts about what you want to do. And what you then do is nearly always the wrong thing to do. Double-check your line, of course, and remember what you want to do with speed and direction. Then bring back the putter and concentrate on keeping the clubhead square.

The longer you take to putt, the longer the other golfers must wait. That can create tension in the minds and muscles, which will produce what we have worked to prevent: three-putting.

Let's Go to the Practice Green

The biggest mistake you can make as a high handicapper or as a low handicapper, I believe, is to go out onto a golf course for a round and stroll right by the practice green. You are almost automatically dooming yourself to a fat score if you say you don't have time to practice your putting stroke. Here is a checklist that I use to get my putting stroke back into its groove:

☐ Stand about 10 feet from a cup and take the proper grip. Swing at a ball that is not there. Get the feel of the putterhead.

☐ Place six balls in a row about nine feet from the cup. Putt each ball without thinking about direction or speed, not caring where the ball stops. Review in your mind the mechanics of the pendulum putting motion. Concentrate on bringing the clubhead back square, impacting the ball with the clubhead square, then following through

115

From 20 feet away, concentrate on tapping balls within the
48-inch circle of balls.

From two feet away, concentrate on the pendulum motion, keeping the clubhead square and "dropping" the clubhead into the cup.

with the clubhead square to the target line. Concentrate on what is happening at the near end of the putt.

☐ Concentrate next on the putt's far end—its speed and direction. Place six balls 15 feet from the cup. Aim to stop each ball within a 48-inch circle around the cup. Try to stop five of six within the circle.

☐ Link together the near-end mechanics of the putt with the far-end mechanics. Place six balls 20 feet away. Concentrate on speed and direction—the far-end mechanics. Stop five of six within that 48-inch circle. Then place six balls two feet away and concentrate on the pendulum motion and on keeping the clubhead square—the near-end mechanics. Get the feeling that the clubhead is being dropped into the cup. Sink six of six from two feet away and that satisfying rattle of the ball inside the cup will give you the confidence to face the tough ones that you'll face tomorrow—our last day together—when we go to the greens.

Let's Go to the Greens!

You are now playing your first round since you finished the first 17 days of our putting lessons. As you go from green to green, you are going to be looking at an infinite variety of putts. Inch for inch, no two putts are exactly alike. But on the other hand, all putts are either straight or breaking; and all putts are either long, medium or short. Now, while I can't hover over your shoulder and tell you how to stroke each putt, I can look over your shoulder at five putts you will often see—and tell you how to make them.

1. THE LONG STRAIGHT PUTT

Here you must be thinking at least 60 percent speed, no more than 40 percent direction. You are aiming for a wide target—the four-foot-wide circle. Remind yourself that you want the ball to go through the half of the circle that's closest to you so that it at least reaches the hole. Never up, never in. And you would like the ball to ride that straight line as if the line were a groove. So, from the point of view of both speed and direction, hit the ball *firmly*. Bring the clubhead back a good way, swing the club through a good way.

2. THE LONG BREAKING PUTT

Think 40 percent speed, 60 percent direction. The ball must be slowing down at the point where it breaks, so speed is important. But you can only guess at the precise point where the ball will break, so it is more important to direct the ball to the general area where the ball's lack of speed will allow the slope to take it down to your four-foot-wide circle. The key, then, is directing the ball to that general area where the ball will break, not to a specific area. If the ball breaks anywhere in that general area, your chances are good that it will stop within your four-foot-wide circle.

3. MEDIUM PUTTS

On a lot of the shorter par-4 holes, you will often land your approach shot within 12 to 15 feet of the pin. If the putt is straight, you almost certainly will two-putt. Think 60 percent speed, 40 percent direction. Breaking putts are obviously trickier, especially if you hope to one-putt. Think 60 percent direction, 40 percent speed. From this short distance, it should be relatively easy to see where the ball will slow down and start to break downward. Concentrate on getting the ball to that point at close to the correct speed.

4. UPHILL AND DOWNHILL MEDIUM-TO-LONG PUTTS

Most of these putts should be hit with speed 60 percent in mind, direction 40 percent. On uphill putts the key word is oomph. You want to hit the ball so firmly that it will stay on line and get to the hole, but on the other hand you want the ball to stop short of the hole. Why? Because you don't want to putt downhill on your second putt. This is one time where the dictum "never up, never in" does not apply.

On downhill putts remind yourself to hit with less oomph, but aim to stop the ball past the hole if it goes off line. Your second putt will then be the relatively easier uphiller.

5. THE STRAIGHT OR BREAKING SHORT PUTT

A well-aimed chip shot from the apron of the green will often leave you with a makable putt of three to six feet—and a chance to make par or a bogey, which is "par" to high handicappers. On straight putts think 65 percent speed, 35 percent direction. You want to hit the ball firmly so that (1) it does not waver off line and (2) it reaches the hole with enough speed to reach the back edge of the cup. Think "backboard" on the shorter putts—you want the ball to "rebound" off an invisible backboard an inch or two behind the cup, then drop.

On breaking putts of under three feet, ignore the break and go directly for the hole, hitting the ball with enough speed so that it goes through the break. On breaking putts of three or more feet, you must think 50 percent speed, 50 percent direction, concentrating on directing the ball to that spot where you can see that the ball, if it slows down, will drop toward the hole.

On all putts, here are two reminders:

1. Keep the body firm and solid. Even if this happens to be a long putt, trust your arms and hands and the club—not any body action—to roll the ball.

2. Grip the club firmly with the two thumbs. They are the two pressure points. There are two worn spots on the grip of my putter—the spots where I place my thumbs. The thumb pressure is a key to keeping the putterhead square and straight to the target line going back, at impact and coming through.

Flash those two reminders to yourself before each putt. If you do, I guarantee you are going to see fewer three-putt greens on your scorecard.

As I said when we first met, one-putt and two-putt greens are golf's equalizers. When you two-putt your next green, tell yourself that even Jack Nicklaus seldom does any better. And when you one-putt a green, you know that Jack Nicklaus *never* does any better.

About the Authors

Walter Ostroske has been a PGA Teaching Pro for the past 25 years. He has played in numerous tournaments and has written magazine articles on golf instruction. Currently head pro at the Hempstead Golf and Country Club on Long Island, he is a member of the MacGregor Advisory Staff.

John Devaney is the author of more than 25 books and has written hundreds of magazine articles on sports. The former editor of *Sport Magazine*, he is the editor of Harris Publications golf magazines and is an adjunct lecturer at Fordham University.

Walter Ostroske and John Devaney are the authors of the highly successful *Break 100 in 21 Days: A How-to Guide for the Weekend Golfer* and *Correct the 10 Most Common Golf Problems in 10 Days.*

ABOUT THE PHOTOGRAPHER

Aime La Montagne is a successful free-lance photographer living in Palmer, Massachusetts. His golfing photographs have appeared in national magazines.

Three putters determined to erase three-putts from your game:
Left to right, Aime La Montagne, Walter Ostroske, John Devaney.

Improve your game with these comprehensive Perigee golf guides.

Break 100 in 21 Days
A How-to Guide for the Weekend Golfer
by Walter Ostroske and John Devaney
illustrated with over 50 black-and-white photographs
The first easy-to-follow program by a PGA teaching pro for shooting in the 90s and 80s, aimed at the person who plays only ten to twenty times a year.

Correct the 10 Most Common Golf Problems in 10 Days
by Walter Ostroske and John Devaney
illustrated with over 50 black-and-white photographs
The first book to pinpoint and correct the ten most common problems in golfers' swings—in just ten days.

Two-Putt Greens in 18 Days
A How-to Guide for the Weekend Golfer
by Walter Ostroske and John Devaney
illustrated with over 50 black-and-white photographs
An easy-to-use daily program for mastering good putting in just eighteen days.

Golf Games Within the Game
200 Fun Ways Players Can Add Variety and Challenge to Their Game
by Linda Valentine and Margie Hubbard
illustrated with over 25 line drawings
A one-of-a-kind collection of games and bets for added excitement on the golf course, culled from members of more than 8,000 golf clubs across America.

The Whole Golf Catalog
by Rhonda Glenn and Robert R. McCord
illustrated with line drawings and photographs
Lists professional and amateur golf associations, golf museums and archives, instruction camps and tours, sources of golf merchandise, a calendar of important events, and much more.

Golf Rules in Pictures
An Official Publication of the United States Golf Association
introduction by Arnold Palmer
Clearly captioned pictures cover all the rules of golf: scoring, clubs, procedure, hazards, and penalty strokes. Includes the official text of The Rules of Golf approved by the U.S. Golf Association and the Royal and Ancient Golf Club of St. Andrews, Scotland.

Golf Techniques in Pictures
by Michael Brown
illustrated with over 100 line drawings
Chock-full of both fundamental and advanced techniques, this is the most complete handbook for successful swinging, putting, and chipping.

These books are available at your local bookstore or wherever books are sold. Ordering is also easy and convenient. Just call 1-800-631-8571 or send your order to:

The Putnam Publishing Group
390 Murray Hill Parkway, Dept. B
East Rutherford, NJ 07073

____ Break 100 in 21 Days	399-51600-X	$8.95	$11.75
____ Correct the 10 Most Common Golf Problems in 10 Days	399-51656-5	8.95	11.75
____ Two-Putt Greens in 18 Days	399-51747-2	8.95	11.75
____ Golf Games Within the Game	399-51762-6	8.95	11.75
____ The Whole Golf Catalog	399-51623-9	15.95	20.95
____ Golf Rules in Pictures	399-51438-4	7.95	10.50
____ Golf Techniques in Pictures	399-51664-6	7.95	10.50

Subtotal $_____

Postage and handling* $_____

Sales tax (CA, NJ, NY, PA) $_____

Total Amount Due $_____

Payable in U.S. funds (no cash orders accepted). $10.00 minimum for credit card orders.
*Postage and handling: $2.00 for 1 book, 50¢ for each additional book up to a maximum of $4.50.

Enclosed is my ☐ check ☐ money order
Please charge my ☐ Visa ☐ MasterCard ☐ American Express

Card # _____ Expiration date _____

Signature as on charge card _____

Name _____

Address _____

City _____ State _____ Zip _____

Please allow six weeks for delivery. Prices subject to change without notice.

**Wall Street
Main Street
AND THE
Side Street**

For Joseph Johnson,
With best wishes,
Julianne M——
7-12-99